A LIFEGUIDE BIBLE STUDY

JONAH, JOEL & AMOS

Seek the Lord and Live!

13 Studies
for individuals or groups

Doug & Doris Haugen

With Notes for Leaders

INTERVARSITY PRESS
DOWNERS GROVE, ILLINOIS 60515

InterVarsity Press is the book-publishing division of InterVarsity Christian Fellowship, a student movement active on campus at hundreds of universities, colleges and schools of nursing. For information about local and regional activities, write Public Relations Dept., InterVarsity Christian Fellowship, 6400 Schroeder Rd., P.O. Box 7895, Madison, WI 53707-7895.

Distributed in Canada through InterVarsity Press, 860 Denison St., Unit 3, Markham, Ontario L3R 4H1, Canada.

All Scripture quotations, unless otherwise indicated, are taken from the Holy Bible, New International Version. Copyright © *1973, 1978, International Bible Society. Used by permission of Zondervan Bible Publishers.*

Cover photograph: Robert Flesher

ISBN 0-8308-1032-3

Printed in the United States of America

18	17	16	15	14	13	12	11	10	9	8	7	6	5	4	3	2
99	98	97	96	95	94	93	92	91	90	89						

Contents

Getting the Most
from LifeGuide Bible Studies

Many of us long to fill our minds and our lives with Scripture. We desire to be transformed by its message. LifeGuide Bible Studies are designed to be an exciting and challenging way to do just that. They help us to be guided by God's Word in every area of life.

How They Work

LifeGuides have a number of distinctive features. Perhaps the most important is that they are *inductive* rather than *deductive*. They lead us to *discover* what the Bible says rather than *telling* us what it says.

They are also thought provoking. They help us to think about the meaning of the passage so that we can truly understand what the author is saying. The questions require more than one-word answers.

The studies are personal. Questions expose us to the promises, assurances, exhortations and challenges of God's Word. They are designed to allow the Scriptures to renew our minds so that we can be transformed by the Spirit of God. This is the ultimate goal of all Bible study.

The studies are versatile. They are designed for student, neighborhood and church groups. They are also effective for individual study.

How They're Put Together

LifeGuides also have a distinctive format. Each study need take no more than forty-five minutes in a group setting or thirty minutes in personal study—unless you choose to take more time.

The studies can be used within a quarter system in a church and fit well in a semester or trimester system on a college campus. If a guide has more than thirteen studies, it is divided into two or occasionally three parts of approximately twelve studies each.

LifeGuides use a workbook format. Space is provided for writing answers to each question. This is ideal for personal study and allows group members to prepare in advance for the discussion.

The studies also contain leader's notes. They show how to lead a group discussion, provide additional background information on certain questions, give helpful tips on group dynamics and suggest ways to deal with problems which may arise during the discussion. With such helps, someone with little or no experience can lead an effective study.

Suggestions for Individual Study

1. As you begin each study, pray that God will help you to understand and apply the passage to your life.

2. Read and reread the assigned passage to familiarize yourself with what the author is saying. You may want to read through the entire book prior to the first study to get an overview of its contents.

3. A good modern translation of the Bible, rather than the King James Version or a paraphrase, will give you the most help. The New International Version, the New American Standard Bible and the Revised Standard Version are all recommended. However, the questions in this guide are based on the New International Version.

4. Write your answers in the space provided in the study guide. This will help you to express your understanding of the passage clearly.

5. It might be good to have a Bible dictionary handy. Use it to look up any unfamiliar words, names or places.

Suggestions for Group Study

1. Come to the study prepared. Follow the suggestions for individual study mentioned above. You will find that careful preparation will greatly enrich your time spent in group discussion.

2. Participate in the discussion. The leader of your group will not be lecturing but encouraging the members to discuss what they have learned from the passage. The leader will be asking the questions that are found in this guide. Plan to share what God has taught you in your individual study.

3. Stick to the passage being studied. Your answers should be based on the verses which are the focus of the discussion and not on outside authorities such as commentaries or speakers.

4. Be sensitive to the other members of the group. Listen attentively when they share what they have learned. You may be surprised by their insights! Also, be affirming whenever you can. This will encourage some of the more hesitant members of the group to participate.

5. Be careful not to dominate the discussion. We are sometimes so eager to share what we have learned that we leave too little opportunity for others to respond. By all means participate! But allow others to also.

6. Expect God to teach you through the passage being discussed and through the other members. Pray for a profitable time together.

7. If you are the discussion leader, you will find additional suggestions for each study in the leader's notes. These are found at the back of the guide.

Introducing Jonah, Joel & Amos

In "The Great Stone Face" Nathaniel Hawthorne told the story of a rock formation on the side of a mountain that resembled a human face. Legend had it that a truly great man resembling the great stone face would someday come to the nearby town. One boy made it his life's goal to study the face and search for its resemblance in others. Over the years he spent countless hours gazing with wonder at that awesome face. As the boy matured into manhood, and as life's influence molded him, those around him were amazed to see what he had become—the great stone face!

A wise professor once said, "What gets your attention, gets you." This is especially true in the books of Jonah, Joel and Amos. In each book God takes drastic measures to get people's attention. He does so not because he delights in calamity but because he desires our fellowship. No matter who we are—prophet, pagan, or God's own people, he will do whatever is necessary to draw us to himself.

Jonah

Jonah prophesied in the eighth century B.C., during or shortly before the reign of Jeroboam II (793-753 B.C.). God called him to preach to Nineveh, the capital of Assyria, which was the most powerful nation on earth. The more we know about Assyria, the more we understand why Jonah was reluctant to preach there. The Assyrians were a fierce, warring people who often treated their captors ruthlessly. Jonah had good reason to be afraid!

But fear was not the only thing that made Jonah reluctant. His attitude reflects the racial prejudice common in his day. The "chosen people" could not imagine that God could care about other nations—especially one as vile and idolatrous as Assyria. So the book of Jonah becomes a powerful illustration of the fact that God does not want "anyone to perish, but everyone to come to repentance" (2 Pet 3:9).

The story of Jonah has been the subject of much controversy. Many people reject its historicity, preferring to view it as an allegory or parable. However, two things should be noted about this view.

First, few people questioned the historicity of Jonah until the nineteenth century, when liberal scholars launched an attack not only on this book but on every book in the Bible. They objected to its historicity primarily because of the incident of Jonah being swallowed by a fish. However, even from a natural standpoint this incident is quite possible. In his *Introduction to the Old Testament*, R. K. Harrison points out that there are other reliable records of people being swallowed by large fish and surviving.*

Second, Jesus himself viewed the story of Jonah as history (Mt 12:38-41; Lk 11:29-30, 32), comparing it to the greater miracle of his resurrection. Surely those who believe in the latter should have no difficulty believing in the former.

Joel

We know little about the man Joel, other than the fact that his message was geared toward Judah, and he was probably a resident of Jerusalem. The date of his writing is disputed among scholars. While some say Joel prophesied as late as 400 B.C., many believe he was a contemporary of Jonah and Amos.

Joel's prophecy came in the wake of a devastating locust plague. Joel saw this plague as a sign of God's judgment and warned that unless the people returned to the Lord they would face even greater judgment on the day of the Lord. But to those willing to "rend their hearts" he promised great blessings that would more than repay "the years the locusts have eaten" (2:25).

Amos

Although Amos was a farmer from Judah, he prophesied to Israel, the northern kingdom, around 760 B.C. During this period the nation was secure and the upper classes prospered. Archaeological discoveries at Megiddo and Samaria have uncovered carved ivory inlays that were used in the furniture and decorative paneling in the homes of the wealthy. But instead of using their wealth to serve the needy, the upper classes were deaf to their cries. In fact, the wealthy maintained their lifestyle by oppressing the poor.

Although the Israelites continued to worship God, their worship was cold and self-serving. Jeroboam had built temples in Bethel and Dan so the people would worship in the north rather than traveling to Jerusalem. But God viewed this worship as idolatrous and declared, "I hate, I despise your religious feasts; I cannot stand your assemblies. Even though you bring me burnt offerings and grain offerings, I will not accept them" (Amos 5:21-22).

God's judgment came against Israel in the form of famine, drought and plagues. But because the people failed to return to the Lord, Amos prophesied that all but a remnant would be destroyed. Still the Lord pleaded with Israel, "Seek good, not evil, that you may live!" (Amos 5:14).

The books of Jonah, Joel and Amos have a powerful message today. We sometimes run from God's will and need to be brought back. At other times we wander from God's ways and need to return to him. And we often seek the wrong things, forgetting the One who is the only source of true life. These prophets challenge us to forsake anything and everything that hinders our relationship with God. Together they proclaim, "Seek the Lord and live!"

Introduction to the Old Testament (Grand Rapids, Mich.: Eerdmans, 1969), pp. 907-8.

1
Jonah's Disobedience

Jonah 1:1-17

D on't hit your sister!"

Sometimes it takes all the will power we have to obey. Yet how easy it is to do wrong in the first place. We get mad and we react.

That's what it feels like with God sometimes too. He asks us to do things we don't want to do—things that are difficult, uncomfortable or even painful. So politely but firmly we refuse his command and try to put it out of our minds. Yet as Jonah discovered, our disobedience can be even more costly than our obedience.

1. When you were a child, how was your disobedience sometimes more costly than obedience?

2. Read Jonah 1. Nineveh was the capital of Assyria, a nation that was a fierce and powerful enemy of Israel to the northeast. How does Jonah respond to the Lord's command to preach there (vv. 1-3)?

3. Tarshish, traditionally identified as Spain, was over two thousand miles in the opposite direction. While Jonah was journeying to Tarshish, what kinds of thoughts and feelings might he have experienced?

4. Have you ever wanted to run away from something you knew God wanted you to do? Explain.

5. How did the sailors respond to the storm, and how did Jonah respond?

6. How do you think Jonah felt when the captain urged him to call on God for help (v. 6)?

7. Why do the sailors become even more terrified after they hear Jonah's story (vv. 7-10)?

8. Why is it dangerous to disobey God?

9. Jonah acknowledges his guilt in verses 11-12. Do you think he is repentant at this point? Explain.

10. After hearing Jonah's suggestion (v. 12), what new tensions and struggles do the sailors experience (vv. 13-14)?

11. How does God use this calamity to demonstrate his grace and mercy (vv. 15-17)?

12. How does this chapter illustrate the futility of running from God?

2
Jonah's Prayer

Jonah 2:1-10

In the movie *Pinocchio* a kindly woodcutter named Geppetto is swallowed by a whale named Monstro. Inside the dark, damp belly of the whale, Geppetto sits for what seems like an eternity. Then one day the whale violently coughs, and the woodcutter is expelled from his watery grave.

Sound familiar? Every Sunday-school child would recognize this retelling of the story of Jonah. But unlike the Disney movie, Jonah's incredible adventure is not fantasy but fact.

1. What childhood memories do you have of the story of Jonah and the "whale"?

2. Read Jonah 2. Describe the terrible sequence of events after Jonah was thrown overboard (vv. 3, 5, 6a).

3. What initial thoughts and feelings did Jonah have (vv. 3-6)?

4. Describe a situation in which you felt like you were in a deep, dark pit (v. 6), either physically, emotionally or spiritually.

5. What was Jonah's condition when he finally remembered to pray (vv. 1, 7)?

6. Why do you think we sometimes have to sink so low before we remember God?

7. How did these terrifying events affect Jonah's attitude toward God?

8. Why do you think God answered Jonah's prayer (vv. 2, 6, 9-10)?

9. Why can we be confident God will hear our prayers, even if we are suffering the consequences of disobedience?

10. If you were Jonah and had spent three days and nights inside the great fish, how would you feel when you found yourself back on dry land (v. 10)?

11. Describe a difficult situation from which the Lord delivered you.

12. Take time now to thank God for his discipline and his grace. Quietly reaffirm your commitment to obey him.

3
Jonah's Obedience

Jonah 3:1-10

Great revivals have occurred throughout history—among the Jews in the first century, the tribes of Ireland in the fifth century, the Protestants in the sixteenth century and the people of Wales in the twentieth century. Yet one of the greatest revivals of all time occurred hundreds of years before any of these—the amazing revival in Nineveh described in Jonah 3.

1. If a genuine turning to God were to occur in this country, what results would you expect to see?

2. Read Jonah 3. If you were Jonah, how would you feel when the word of the Lord came to you a second time (vv. 1-2)?

3. Assyria was one of the most powerful nations on earth, known especially for its military might and brutality. How would this make it difficult for Jonah to proclaim: "Forty more days and Nineveh will be overturned" (vv. 3-4).

4. Describe a situation in which you found it difficult to share the gospel with an unbeliever.

Why was it difficult?

5. What evidence is there that the Ninevites were sincere in their repentance (vv. 5-9)?

6. How and why does the Lord respond to the Ninevites (v. 10)?

7. What view of God do the Ninevites express in this chapter?

How does their view of God compare with Jonah's view expressed in chapter 2?

8. How does our view of God affect our willingness to turn away from our sins and turn toward God?

9. Describe one area in you life where you feel a need for repentance.

10. What actions can you take to demonstrate the sincerity of your repentance?

4
Jonah's Anger
Jonah 4:1-11

Life is full of minor joys and irritations. Finding a parking place in rush hour can make us very happy. Finding a flat tire when we return can make us miserable. In chapter 4 we discover that Jonah also cared a great deal about life's little ups and downs. Although his petty passions seem amusing, they also invite us to reexamine what we really care about.

1. What little things irritate you or bring you joy?

2. Read Jonah 4. Why was Jonah greatly displeased and angry (vv. 1-3)?

3. Did these things give him any right to be angry (v. 4)? Explain.

4. Evidently the forty days had already passed (3:10). Why then do you think Jonah still waited to see what would happen to the city (v. 5)?

5. How does the Lord use the vine as an object lesson for Jonah (vv. 6-11)?

6. In what ways are we sometimes more concerned about petty things than about those under God's judgment?

7. What can we do to begin seeing things more from God's perspective?

8. How would you summarize the primary message of the book of Jonah?

9. In your life, how have you seen God demonstrate the qualities Jonah mentions in 4:2?

10. How does God's treatment of you motivate you to reach out to those who don't know him?

5
The Locust Invasion

Joel 1:1-20

A crisis can capture anyone's attention. But our response to a crisis can vary greatly from person to person. Some become bitter and hardened. Others quietly endure but learn nothing from the experience. A few, however, find their lives are purified, deepened and strengthened.

In Joel 1 a major crisis has occurred—a swarm of locusts has invaded the land, with devastating results. In the aftermath of the devastation, Joel appears with a word from the Lord. His word still has the power to purify those who hear it.

1. What is the most traumatic event you have seen during your lifetime? Explain.

2. Read Joel 1. Describe the devastation left by the locust plague.

3. How will the plague affect the drunkards (v. 5), the priests (vv. 9, 13) and the farmers (v. 11)?

Why do you think these groups are singled out?

4. "Has anything like this ever happened in your days or in the days of your forefathers?" (v. 2). Why do you think Joel asks the elders this question?

5. In what ways does God discipline his people today, either individually or corporately?

6. What is the difference between God's discipline and the problems anyone may have?

7. Joel commands the elders to tell their children and grandchildren about the dramatic locust invasion (v. 3). Why is this necessary?

8. Joel compares the people of Judah to a virgin mourning for her husband (v. 8). What does this metaphor say about the depth of relationship between God and his people?

9. No greater calamity could befall Judah than the cessation of daily sacrifice (vv. 9, 13), for that was the sign of God's covenant relationship. What was God's purpose in doing this?

10. In verses 13-14 Joel calls the people to repent. How are they to demonstrate their repentance?

11. Why is each of these commands important?

12. In what meaningful ways can we express our repentance today, both individually and corporately?

6
Return to the Lord!

Joel 2:1-27

In order to get to the roses, we must first go through the thorns. The teaching of Joel in the first two chapters is hard. But roses—in the form of the promises of God—lie ahead. Because he loves us, the Father disciplines us when we wander from him. The warnings we see here are God's last resort to bring his people to true repentance—a *heart* relationship rather than one of empty ritual. As we read this chapter, we too must face questions of the heart.

1. How do we sometimes serve God outwardly rather than from the heart?

2. Read Joel 2:1-17. Why does Joel urge the people to blow the trumpet and sound the alarm (v. 1)?

3. Do you think Joel is describing a literal locust invasion in chapter 2 or an army invasion which simply resembles a swarm of locusts? Explain.

4. Joel compares the invasion to "the day of the LORD" (1:15; 2:1-2, 11). What can we learn about that day from these verses?

5. How can the day of the Lord be a warning against spiritual complacency?

6. "Even now," what hope does the Lord offer his people, and why (vv. 12-14)?

What does it mean to return to the Lord with all our heart (v. 12)?

7. Again Joel calls for a "holy fast . . . a sacred assembly" (v. 15). What is significant about the people he singles out in verses 16-17?

8. How do verses 12-17 help us understand the meaning of repentance?

9. In what ways would you like to renew your commitment to the Lord?

10.   Read Joel 2:18-27. If his people repent, what promises does the Lord make them (vv. 18-27)?

11.   How would these promises repay them for "the years the locusts have eaten" (v. 25)?

12.   How have you experienced God's healing through the act of repentance?

13.   Take time to "praise the name of the LORD your God" for the wonders he has worked for you (v. 26).

7
The Day of the Lord

Joel 2:28—3:21

Christians long for that great and final day when the Lord will return. But the day of the Lord will not be the same for everyone. For some it will be a day of indescribable joy and blessing. For others it will be a day of judgment and terror. In this final section of his book, Joel looks at both aspects of the day of the Lord. As you read his words, try to discover why people's experience of the Lord will be so radically different.

1. When you think of the Lord's return, what images come to mind?

2. Read Joel 2:28—3:21. According to verses 28-31, what signs will precede the "coming of the great and dreadful day of the LORD"?

3. In verses 28-29 the Lord promises to pour out his Spirit. What is significant about the people he mentions and the experiences they will have?

4. As the dreadful day of the Lord approaches, what offer does he make (v. 32)?

What connection is there (if any) between this offer and the promise of his Spirit?

---

5. Peter claimed Joel's prophecy was fulfilled on the day of Pentecost (Acts 2:17-21, 38-40). How then does Joel's promise of the Spirit and salvation apply to us?

---

6. What have the nations done to provoke the Lord's judgment (3:1-8)?

How will he repay them?

---

7. The Lord commands the nations to prepare for war (v. 9). How does their battle relate to the Lord's judgment (vv. 9-16)?

---

8. Joel describes the Lord as a lion, a thunderstorm, a refuge and a stronghold (v. 16). What do these images reveal about the God we serve?

9. What blessings does the Lord promise his people (vv. 16-21)?

---

10. In his covenant promise with Abraham, God said, "I will bless those who bless you, and whoever curses you I will curse; and all peoples on earth will be blessed through you" (Gen 12:3). How does the Lord fulfill that promise in this chapter?

---

11. What has Joel taught you about preparing for the day of the Lord?

---

12. What steps do you need to take in order to be prepared?

8
The Lord Roars from Zion
Amos 1:1—2:16

Picture this if you will. It is about the middle of the eighth century B.C. People are flocking to the worship center at Bethel, people whom we might call "upper middle class." The design of the building is very appealing. The choirs are polished. Several brilliant orators are at hand. It feels good to come here—uplifting music, beautiful surroundings and comforting words. There is even opportunity for the people to placate their consciences by bringing offerings.

But wait a minute! Who is that seedy-looking character? He speaks like a shepherd; he looks like a shepherd; he even smells like a shepherd—but he sure doesn't sound like a shepherd!

1. Recall something you never thought would happen to you. How did you feel when it *did* happen?

2. Read Amos 1:1—2:5. How does 1:2 set the tone for Amos's message?

3. Damascus, Gaza, Tyre, Edom, Ammon and Moab all represented enemies of Israel. How would the Israelites feel as they heard prophecies against these nations (1:3—2:3)?

4. Describe how the people might respond as the prophecy turns to Judah, the southern kingdom (2:4-5)?

5. Read Amos 2:6-16. How might their attitude change as they heard the words, "For three sins of *Israel,* even for four, I will not turn back my wrath" (2:6)?

6. Do you think it is characteristic of human nature to assume that judgment will always fall on someone else? Explain.

7. The statement "For three sins . . . even for four" emphasizes God's patience before pronouncing judgment. What kinds of sin do the pagan nations have in common (1:3—2:3)?

8. How are Judah's sins different from those of the pagan nations (2:4-5)?

9. Amos cites a variety of sins of which Israel is guilty (vv. 6-8, 12). How would you categorize their sins?

10. How are the righteous, the needy, the poor and the oppressed mistreated?

11. As Christians, what can we do to bring relief and justice to such people?

12. How are Israel's sins all the more serious in light of their history (vv. 9-11)?

13. What graphic images does the Lord use to describe his judgment of Israel (vv. 13-16)?

14. How can Amos's warnings to Israel keep us from being presumptuous about our status as God's children?

9
Israel's Punishment

Amos 3:1-15

Awell-known insurance company uses cartoons to advertise their product. One cartoon pictures a piano falling from an upper-story window toward an unsuspecting man below. As it speeds toward its destination, a friend politely asks: "By the way, what's the name of your insurance company?" "Acme insurance, of course," the man replies. "Why do you ask?"

Disaster often comes unexpectedly. The people of Israel were wealthy, self-centered and complacent. Little did they realize that the full weight of God's judgment was about to fall on them.

1. Why do many people have difficulty believing in God as judge?

2. Read Amos 3:1-15. The Israelites were confident that Yahweh was their God and they were his chosen people. But how had they misunderstood that call (vv. 1-2)?

3. "Privilege brings responsibility." Give an example of how this is true for us as Christians.

4. In verses 3-6 Amos asks several rhetorical questions. How would you summarize what he is trying to say in these verses?

5. Why do you think the Lord does nothing without revealing his plan to the prophets (v. 7)?

6. Why does the Lord summon pagan nations to assemble on the mountains of Samaria (vv. 9-10)?

What does this say about Israel's morality and lifestyle in comparison with the pagan nations?

7. How would the Lord's judgment against Israel fit their crimes (vv. 10-11, 15)?

8. What kind of "salvation" could these Israelites expect (v. 12)?

9. According to the law, people in danger could find refuge by grasping the horns of the altar (see 1 Kings 1:50). How and why would this change (vv. 13-14)?

10. Try to view this chapter from the perspective of those who were oppressed by the wealthy. How would you feel as you heard Amos's prophecy?

11. What does this chapter teach us about God's character?

12. What does this chapter teach us about our responsibility as people of God?

10
Prepare to Meet Your God!

Amos 4:1-13

In 1741 Jonathan Edwards preached his most famous sermon: "Sinners in the Hands of an Angry God." After using vivid imagery to make non-Christians feel the horror of their position, Edwards concluded: "Therefore, let every one that is out of Christ now awake and fly from the wrath to come!" God used that sermon to bring a powerful awakening to the town of Enfield, in New England.

The prophet Amos preaches a similar sermon in this chapter. After warning Israel repeatedly to return to the Lord, he now declares: "Prepare to meet your God!"

1. Recall a time when you wandered from God. What brought you back?

2. Read Amos 4:1-13. The area of Bashan was noted for its fat, sleek cattle. In light of this, how would you describe the lifestyle of the women of Israel (v. 1)?

3. How does this lifestyle contrast with the judgment the Lord swears to bring upon them (vv. 2-3)?

4. Bethel and Gilgal were centers of worship for the northern kingdom (1 Kings 12:26-33; Hos 4:15). What was sinful about Israel's worship at these places (vv. 4-5)?

5. How can we keep our worship from becoming empty ritual?

6. What words would you use to describe each of the judgments the Lord brought on Israel (vv. 6-11)?

7. How do these judgments compare to the curses for disobedience described in Deuteronomy 28:15-48?

8. What is the purpose of the judgments that have come upon Israel?

What method does the writer use to emphasize this purpose?

9. Why do you think we sometimes need to be disciplined repeatedly before we will return to God?

10. God's tenderness, even in the midst of judgment, is evident in the repeated words, "yet you have not returned to me" (vv. 6, 8, 9, 11). How have you experienced God's grace in the midst of discipline?

11. Amos proclaims to Israel, "Prepare to meet your God" (v. 12). In light of this chapter, what kind of "meeting" could Israel expect this to be?

12. The chapter closes with a brief hymn describing the God Israel would meet in judgment (v. 13). What do we learn about God from each aspect of Amos's description?

Take a few minutes to worship God, using this hymn as the basis for your prayers.

11
Seek the Lord and Live!

Amos 5:1—6:14

Success, wealth, power, prestige—these are eagerly sought by many today. People are willing to sacrifice their marriages, their families and even their health to obtain these goals. But in the end most discover that the rewards were not worth the cost. How tragic! In chapters 5 and 6 Amos tells us how to avoid this tragedy in our lives—"Seek the Lord and live!"

1. Why do you think people are willing to sacrifice so much to obtain the things mentioned above?

2. Read Amos 5. A *lament* (v. 1) was a song or poem mourning someone's death. How does Amos portray the death of Israel (v. 2)?

Why do you think he compares Israel to a virgin?

3. What has Israel done to deserve the Lord's judgment (vv. 7, 10, 11, 12)?

4. What warnings of judgment does the Lord give in this chapter?

5. How does the Lord plead with Israel in verses 4, 6, 14 and 15?

In this context, what would it mean for Israel to *seek* the Lord?

6. If Amos were prophesying today, how would he expect us to *hate evil* and *love good* (v. 15)?

7. How were the Israelites mistaken about the day of the Lord (v. 18-20)?

8. Amos uses scathing language in verses 21-23. How might this prepare his audience to hear the message of verse 24?

9. Read Amos 6. How does Amos portray the Israelites in verses 1-6?

10. In their complacency and security, Israel failed to grieve over the ruin of their nation (v. 6). What should grieve us today about our personal lives, our church and our nation?

11. How does the Lord promise to repay those who are complacent and proud (vv. 7-14)?

12. Take time to pray about those things that cause you to grieve. Ask the Lord to help you seek his will in these areas.

12
Five Visions (Part 1)
Amos 7:1–8:14

Lt is easy to side with Amos. After all, his prophecies are part of the Bible! But put yourself in Israel's place. How would you have responded if a farmer came to town and began announcing visions of judgment? In chapters 7—9 we will look at five of Amos's visions and one fairly typical response.

1. Have you ever been confronted by a street preacher who warned of God's judgment? If so, how did you respond?

2. Read Amos 7. What three visions of judgment does the Lord show Amos in this chapter (vv. 1, 4, 7)?

3. Why does the Lord "relent" regarding the first two visions (vv. 1-6)?

4. How can the Lord's response to Amos's prayers motivate us to pray for our nation?

5. In the third vision the wall had been "plumb-line-built" and was being subjected to a plumb-line test. Why was this an appropriate analogy for Israel?

6. J. A. Motyer writes: "People who are brought near to God cannot avoid being tested and judged."* Do you agree or disagree with his statement? Explain.

7. In verses 10-17, Amos undergoes his own "plumb-line" test. What temptations might he have experienced?

8. In what situations are you tempted to compromise your beliefs or convictions?

How can Amos's response to Amaziah be an example to us (vv. 10-17)?

9. Read Amos 8. A basket of ripe fruit (v. 1) was normally associated with the joys of summer harvest. But in this instance, how does it become a picture of judgment (v. 2)?

10. How does Amos describe the lifestyle of those who are ripe for judgment (vv. 4-6)?

11. How does he describe the "harvest" they will experience (vv. 3-14)?

12. Earlier the Lord had sent famine to bring Israel to repentance (4:6-8). Because they did not return to him, what kind of "famine" was inevitable (8:11-12)?

13. Even though we live in a country where we can freely read the Bible, how does this "famine" evidence itself among God's people?

What can we do about it?

*J. A. Motyer, *The Day of the Lion* (Downers Grove, Ill.: InterVarsity Press, 1974), p. 160.

13
Five Visions
(Part 2)
Amos 9:1-15

Hope is one of the three greatest gifts. It can lift our broken spirits, strengthen our feeble bodies and transform our darkest moments into light-hearted praise. Up to this point Amos has offered little hope to Israel. But in this final chapter, as the pace toward destruction quickens, he brings his prophecy to a surprising conclusion—one that is full of hope, promise and a renewed vision of God.

1. How does hope differ from wishful or "positive" thinking?

2. Read Amos 9. In this fifth vision Amos sees the Lord himself standing by the temple altar (v. 1). What happens to the temple and the people assembled there?

How does Amos describe the fate of those who try to escape (vv. 1-4)?

3. How do you think the description of the Lord in verses 5-6 relates to the pronouncements of the previous verses?

What is your response to these words?

4. The Israelites thought they were superior to other nations because God chose them and delivered them from Egypt. Why would they be shocked by verse 7 and the first part of verse 8?

5. What glimmer of hope does Amos offer the house of Jacob (vv. 8-10)?

Upon what foundation is this hope built?

6. Suddenly Israel's glimmer of hope begins to shine with intense brightness (vv. 11-15). How does Amos's final prophecy contrast with what he has said before?

7. After hearing all of Amos's harsh words, how would this prophecy make you feel if you were an Israelite?

8. Describe a time in your life or in the life of your church when the Lord restored what was in ruins (v. 11).

9. How do verses 11-15 help to balance the picture of God we have seen in this book?

10. How can this portrait of God give us hope even when things seem hopeless?

11. What have you appreciated most about studying Jonah, Joel and Amos?

What is the most important insight you have gained from these books?

Leader's Notes

Leading a Bible discussion can be an enjoyable and rewarding experience. But it can also be *scary*—especially if you've never done it before. If this is your feeling, you're in good company. When God asked Moses to lead the Israelites out of Egypt, he replied, "O Lord, please send someone else to do it!" (Ex 4:13).

When Solomon became king of Israel, he felt the task was far beyond his abilities. "I am only a little child and do not know how to carry out my duties. . . . Who is able to govern this great people of yours?" (1 Kings 3:7, 9).

When God called Jeremiah to be a prophet, he replied, "Ah, Sovereign LORD, . . . I do not know how to speak; I am only a child" (Jer 1:6).

The list goes on. The apostles were "unschooled, ordinary men" (Acts 4:13). Timothy was young, frail and frightened. Paul's "thorn in the flesh" made him feel weak. But God's response to all of his servants—including you—is essentially the same: "My grace is sufficient for you" (2 Cor 12:9). Relax. God helped these people in spite of their weaknesses, and he can help you in spite of your feelings of inadequacy.

There is another reason why you should feel encouraged. Leading a Bible discussion is not difficult if you follow certain guidelines. You don't need to be an expert on the Bible or a trained teacher. The suggestions listed below should enable you to effectively and enjoyably fulfill your role as leader.

Preparing to Lead

1. Ask God to help you understand and apply the passage to your own life. Unless this happens, you will not be prepared to lead others. Pray too for the various members of the group. Ask God to give you an enjoyable and profitable time together studying his Word.

2. As you begin each study, read and reread the assigned Bible passage to familiarize yourself with what the author is saying. In the case of book studies, you may want to read through the entire book prior to the first study. This will give you a helpful overview of its contents.

3. This study guide is based on the New International Version of the Bible. It will help you and the group if you use this translation as the basis for your study and discussion. Encourage others to use the NIV also, but allow them the freedom to use whatever translation they prefer.

4. Carefully work through each question in the study. Spend time in meditation and reflection as you formulate your answers.

5. Write your answers in the space provided in the study guide. This will help you to express your understanding of the passage clearly.

6. It might help you to have a Bible dictionary handy. Use it to look up any unfamiliar words, names or places. (For additional help on how to study a passage, see chapter five of *Leading Bible Discussions,* IVP.)

7. Once you have finished your own study of the passage, familiarize yourself with the leader's notes for the study you are leading. These are designed to help you in several ways. First, they tell you the purpose the study guide author had in mind while writing the study. Take time to think through how the study questions work together to accomplish that purpose. Second, the notes provide you with additional background information or comments on some of the questions. This information can be useful if people have difficulty understanding or answering a question. Third, the leader's notes can alert you to potential problems you may encounter during the study.

8. If you wish to remind yourself of anything mentioned in the leader's notes, make a note to yourself below that question in the study.

Leading the Study

1. Begin the study on time. Unless you are leading an evangelistic Bible study, open with prayer, asking God to help you to understand and apply the passage.

2. Be sure that everyone in your group has a study guide. Encourage them to prepare beforehand for each discussion by working through the questions in the guide.

3. At the beginning of your first time together, explain that these studies are meant to be discussions not lectures. Encourage the members of the group to participate. However, do not put pressure on those who may be hesitant to speak during the first few sessions.

4. Read the introductory paragraph at the beginning of the discussion. This will orient the group to the passage being studied.

5. Read the passage aloud if you are studying one chapter or less. You may choose to do this yourself, or someone else may read if he or she has been asked to do so prior to the study. Longer passages may occasionally be read in parts at different times during the study. Some studies may cover several chapters. In such cases reading aloud would probably take too much time, so the group members should simply read the assigned passages prior to the study.

6. As you begin to ask the questions in the guide, keep several things in mind. First, the questions are designed to be used just as they are written. If you wish, you may simply read them aloud to the group. Or you may prefer to express them in your own words. However, unnecessary rewording of the questions is not recommended.

Second, the questions are intended to guide the group toward understanding and applying the *main idea* of the passage. The author of the guide has stated his or her view of this central idea in the *purpose* of the study in the leader's notes. You should try to understand how the passage expresses this idea and how the study questions work together to lead the group in that direction.

There may be times when it is appropriate to deviate from the study guide. For example, a question may have already been answered. If so, move on to the next question. Or someone may raise an important question not covered in the guide. Take time to discuss it! The important thing is to use discretion. There may be many routes you can travel to reach the goal of the study. But the easiest route is usually the one the author has suggested.

7. Avoid answering your own questions. If necessary, repeat or rephrase them until they are clearly understood. An eager group quickly becomes passive and silent if they think the leader will do most of the talking.

8. Don't be afraid of silence. People may need time to think about the question before formulating their answers.

9. Don't be content with just one answer. Ask, "What do the rest of you think?" or "Anything else?" until several people have given answers to the question.

10. Acknowledge all contributions. Try to be affirming whenever possible. Never reject an answer. If it is clearly wrong, ask, "Which verse led you to that conclusion?" or again, "What do the rest of you think?"

11. Don't expect every answer to be addressed to you, even though this will probably happen at first. As group members become more at ease, they will begin to truly interact with each other. This is one sign of a healthy discussion.

12. Don't be afraid of controversy. It can be very stimulating. If you don't resolve an issue completely, don't be frustrated. Move on and keep it in mind for later. A subsequent study may solve the problem.

13. Stick to the passage under consideration. It should be the source for answering the questions. Discourage the group from unnecessary cross-referencing. Likewise, stick to the subject and avoid going off on tangents.

14. Periodically summarize what the *group* has said about the passage. This helps to draw together the various ideas mentioned and gives continuity to the study. But don't preach.

15. Conclude your time together with conversational prayer. Be sure to ask God's help to apply those things which you learned in the study.

16. End on time.

Many more suggestions and helps are found in *Leading Bible Discussions* (IVP). Reading and studying through that would be well worth your time.

Components of Small Groups

A healthy small group should do more than study the Bible. There are four components you should consider as you structure your time together.

Nurture. Being a part of a small group should be a nurturing and edifying experience. You should grow in your knowledge and love of God and each other. If we are to properly love God, we must know and keep his commandments (Jn 14:15). That is why Bible study should be a foundational part of your small group. But you can be nurtured by other things as well. You can memorize Scripture, read and discuss a book, or occasionally listen to a tape of a good speaker.

Community. Most people have a need for close friendships. Your small group can be an excellent place to cultivate such relationships. Allow time for informal interaction before and after the study. Have a time of sharing during the meeting. Do fun things together as a group, such as a potluck supper or a picnic. Have someone bring refreshments to the meeting. Be creative!

Worship. A portion of your time together can be spent in worship and prayer. Praise God together for who he is. Thank him for what he has done and is doing in your lives and in the world. Pray for each other's needs. Ask God to help you to apply what you have learned. Sing hymns together.

Mission. Many small groups decide to work together in some form of outreach. This can be a practical way of applying what you have learned. You can host a series of evangelistic discussions for your friends or neighbors. You can visit people at a home for the elderly. Help a widow with cleaning or repair jobs around her home. Such projects can have a transforming influence on your group.

For a detailed discussion of the nature and function of small groups, read *Small Group Leaders' Handbook* or *Good Things Come in Small Groups* (both from IVP).

Leader's Notes
Study 1. Jonah's Disobedience. Jonah 1:1-17.
Purpose: To discover that disobedience can be even more costly than obedience.

Question 1. Almost every study begins with an "approach" question, which is meant to be asked before the passage is read. These questions are important for several reasons.

First, they help the group to warm up to each other. No matter how well a group may know each other, there is always a stiffness that needs to be overcome before people will begin to talk openly. A good question will break the ice.

Second, approach questions get people thinking along the lines of the topic of the study. Most people will have lots of different things going on in their minds (dinner, an important meeting coming up, how to get the car fixed) that will have nothing to do with the study. A creative question will get their attention and draw them into the discussion.

Third, approach questions can reveal where our thoughts or feelings need to be transformed by Scripture. This is why it is especially important not to read the passage before the approach question is asked. The passage will tend to color the honest reactions people would otherwise give because they are of course supposed to think the way the Bible does. Giving honest responses to various issues before they find out what the Bible says may help them to see where their thoughts or attitudes need to be changed.

Questions 2-3. It isn't necessary to suppose Jonah thought he could actually flee from the Lord. Sometimes our actions aren't logical, especially when we try to run away from God's will. Jonah simply wanted to get as far away from Nineveh as possible.

It might help the group if you locate Nineveh, Joppa and Tarshish on a map. If you don't have a large map of Bible lands, you may wish to photocopy a smaller one for each of the group members.

Question 5. The sailors were polytheists and didn't know whose god had been offended or why. So in their fear each one cried out to his favorite deity.

Throughout this chapter it is interesting to note how the pagan sailors seem far more concerned about obedience than Jonah.

Question 6. Because Jonah was running from the Lord, the suggestion that he pray to the Lord would have pricked his conscience. From Jonah's perspective (and ours) the captain's command was full of irony.

Question 7. The sailors may have viewed the sea as uncreated, a remnant of the original chaos. Their chief god, Baal, was a sky god. To hear, therefore, that Jonah's God was the God of heaven, who also made the sea and the land, terrified them. This God was more powerful than any they had imagined.

Question 9. There is a difference between repentance and mere resignation. Was Jonah merely resigned to the fact that he must die for his sin, or did he have a change of heart at this point? The text doesn't tell us, but it is interesting to speculate at this point.

Question 11. God's grace is demonstrated not only to Jonah but also to the sailors, who were awed by what they had witnessed.

Study 2. Jonah's Prayer. Jonah 2:1-10.

Purpose: To learn that even in the darkest circumstances God hears and answers our prayers.

Question 2. This question is designed to help the group imagine the sequence of events Jonah experienced—being thrown into the raging sea (v. 3), having the waves break against him (v. 3), being engulfed by the water (v. 4), having seaweed wrapped around his head (v. 5), being swallowed by the fish (1:17) and then descending in this watery grave to "the roots of the mountains" (v. 6). Each of these would have added to his terror and feelings of helplessness.

Question 3. Notice that Jonah feels both forsaken ("I have been banished from your sight") and hopeful ("I will look again toward your holy temple").

Question 4. This could be a threatening question for some, so be sure not to pressure anyone into answering it.

Question 8. It is God's nature to seek those who run from him and to save those who turn to him. In Jonah's words, "Salvation comes from the LORD" (v. 9).

Question 9. Throughout Scripture God promises to hear those who repent and turn their hearts toward him. (For example, see 1 Jn 1:9.)

Question 10. Remember that Jesus compares Jonah's experience to his own resurrection (Mt 12:38-41; Lk 11:29-30, 32). Jonah would have felt like a man raised from the dead.

Study 3. Jonah's Obedience. Jonah 3:1-10.
Purpose: To learn about genuine repentance from both Jonah and the Ninevites.

Question 2. Try to see the humor as well as the seriousness in verses 1-2. After all that Jonah had experienced, these words would have been the Lord's way of saying: "*Now* are you willing to obey me?" Jonah's response this time was an unhesitating, "YES, SIR!"

Question 3. Help the group to focus on both Assyria's might (they were considered very difficult to overthrow) and their brutality (what would they do to someone like Jonah who proclaimed their destruction?).

Verse 3 mentions that "Now Nineveh was a very important city—a visit required three days." Modern archaeology has shown that the inner wall had a length of almost eight miles. Still, this is quite smaller than a three-day journey. It is probable that Jonah was referring to greater Nineveh, the area that included the entire administrative district.

Question 5. The book of Jonah was probably written during the period of Assyrian weakness between the death of Adad-nirari III (793-753 B.C.) and the beginning of the reign of Tiglath-pileser III in 745 B.C. During this period Assyria was in a life-and-death struggle with tribes to the north and feared for its survival. This may help to account for the fact that the people so readily accepted Jonah's message, although this explanation is not meant to detract from the miraculous nature of what happened.

Question 7. Look at the view of God expressed by their actions as well as by their words.

The Ninevites were polytheists, but their national god was Ashur. Yet behind most polytheistic religions lies a belief in a supreme god capable of exerting his will over all others. We aren't told whether the Ninevites rejected their other deities, but it is clear that they recognized the existence and power of the Supreme God.

Questions 9-10. These questions might cause some members of the group to feel uncomfortable. You might put them at ease if you mention that they don't have to reveal any deep, dark secrets but simply identify one area where they need or desire to change. After all, as Christians we are continually in the process of change as we become more like Jesus Christ.

Study 4. Jonah's Anger. Jonah 4:1-11.
Purpose: To realize that we are sometimes more concerned about petty things than about people under God's judgment.

Questions 2-3. Jonah is one of the most amusing characters in the Bible.

Throughout this chapter his actions are pathetic and humorous. In verses 1-5 he is greatly displeased and angry with God for being so kind and gracious! Help the group to see some of the humor in this chapter.

Question 4. In any narrative portion of Scripture we need to use our imaginations in order to get the full impact of what is taking place. In verse 5 it is helpful to imagine Jonah's mood. The Lord had already decided not to destroy Nineveh—and Jonah knew this. Therefore, his actions are simply stubborn and childish. He goes outside the city to pout and to wait for something he wishes would happen but which he knows will not happen.

Questions 5-6. Jonah is an emotional roller coaster throughout this chapter. First he is angry and wants to die because the Lord decided not to destroy Nineveh. Next he becomes very happy because of the comforting shade of a vine. Then he wants to die again because the vine is destroyed. What a warped sense of values! He would have been happy about Nineveh's destruction, but he wanted to die because of a silly vine's destruction. The Lord gently exposes how mixed up Jonah's values are.

Question 7. Jonah was not wrong to feel sad about the vine—although his reaction was a bit extreme! Likewise, there's nothing wrong with our being concerned about the smaller matters of life. But like Jonah we sometimes have a misplaced sense of values. We care a great deal about a wrecked automobile or a broken television, but we often demonstrate no concern for those who die daily without food or without Christ.

Question 8. In this question help the group to think of ways we can reorient our thinking and our feelings. For example, we might take a fresh look at what Scripture teaches about those who are lost. Or we could read missions-related books or missionary biographies.

Question 10. If you have time, you may wish to discuss practical ways of reaching out to people who don't know Christ. For example, you could begin praying for lost friends or start an evangelistic Bible study. The group might even discuss how in small ways each day our actions and words can make the gospel more attractive to people.

Study 5. The Locust Invasion. Joel 1:1-20.

Purpose: To realize that true repentance requires action.

Questions 2-3. These questions overlap somewhat, moving from a general overview of the devastation to some of its specific effects on the people in the land.

Witnesses of similar plagues in the 1930's tell of dark clouds of locusts cutting off the sunlight, stopping trains on the tracks and wiping out entire fields overnight. This would have a devastating effect on an agrarian society.

"The supplies of wine for the wealthy and the rich would be cut off by the plague. The farmers would no longer be able to 'sit under one's vine and fig tree,' the sign of prosperity" (Derward Deere, *The Wycliffe Bible Commentary*, ed. Charles F. Pfeiffer [Chicago: Moody Press, 1962], p. 821).

Question 4. Joel seems to be saying that this is no ordinary event. Rather, it is so extraordinary that the people should recognize it as God's judgment. It is God's way of getting their attention and disciplining them for their sin.

Questions 5-6. These questions cannot be answered from the text, but they are still important. Whenever we are dealing with Old Testament passages that have no *direct* application to us today, we must look for *parallels* between our situation and theirs. These questions look for such parallels between God's disciplining the people of Judah and his disciplining his people today. Possible references for further discussion include Proverbs 3:11-12, 1 Peter 1:6-7 and Hebrews 12:7-11.

Question 7. This kind of oral tradition ("tell it to your children, and let your children tell it to their children") is common in many cultures. When Alex Haley was doing research in Africa for *Roots,* he spoke to a local "griot" who narrated oral history for over three days without repeating himself, echoing what Hayley had heard over the many years of his boyhood! Such history warned the younger generations against repeating the mistakes of the past.

Question 9. Sacrifices had been offered for hundreds of years (since the time of Abraham) and provided a tremendous sense of security for God's people. The cessation of sacrifice indicated that there was a serious breach in the covenant relationship. Why continue the symbol if the reality no longer existed!

Question 10. Sackcloth (v. 13) was a garment of camel or goat's hair wrapped around the loins, typically signifying mourning. Evidence indicates that it also could have looked like a corn sack with openings for the head, arms and legs. Fasting (v. 14) was also associated with mourning (see 2 Sam 12:16).

Study 6. Return to the Lord! Joel 2:1-27.

Purpose: To realize that true repentance is a matter of the heart and results in blessing.

Question 2. The trumpet was made from a ram's horn and was used to call people to worship, to battle or (as in this case) to warn them of imminent danger.

Question 3. Different opinions exist regarding the interpretation of chapter

2. Some commentators view it as a continuation of the description of the locust invasion in chapter 1. Others suggest it describes a future army which is to attack Israel on the day of the Lord. Notice, however, that the locust invasion in chapter 1 has passed, while the invasion in chapter 2 seems to occur in the future (v. 2).

Questions 5-6. Traditionally the Hebrews viewed the "day of the Lord" as a time when his faithful followers would be blessed and his enemies punished. Joel, however, describes it as a day of destruction, darkness and gloom.

Although there will be only one final day of the Lord, there are many events throughout history that are manifestations of God's judgment and therefore resemble the day of the Lord. The locust invasion in chapter 1 and the subsequent invasion in chapter 2 fall into this category.

Question 6. Notice that hope is offered if the people will return to the Lord with all their *heart* (v. 12). In Hebrew, *heart* denotes the center of life, "the locus of emotions, personality, intellect, sensibility and will" (Derward Deere, *The Wycliffe Bible Commentary,* ed. Charles F. Pfeiffer [Chicago: Moody Press, 1962], p. 823).

Rending one's garments (v. 13) was a sign of mourning, grief or displeasure (see Acts 14:14).

Question 7. Fasting and gathering for a sacred assembly occurs elsewhere in the Old Testament. For example, when Jehoshaphat became afraid at the advance of an army from Edom, he "resolved to inquire of the LORD, and he proclaimed a fast for all Judah. The people of Judah came together to seek help from the LORD" (2 Chron 20:3-4).

The people Joel singles out are from every age group (elders and children). Those who normally would rejoice (bride and bridegroom) are now called to fast and to join in the solemn mood (v. 16). There is also a note of urgency—even the bride and bridegroom are not to wait for the wedding ceremony. Everyone must come immediately!

Questions 10-11. Notice that many of these promises reverse the devastation brought on by the locust plague (see chap. 1).

Study 7. The Day of the Lord. Joel 2:28—3:21.

Purpose: To discover why people's experience of the day of the Lord will be so different.

Question 2. Joel states that the signs will occur both in heaven ("the sun will be turned to darkness and the moon to blood") and on earth ("blood and fire and billows of smoke"). The blood, fire and smoke may be the result of warfare.

Question 3. Under the Old Covenant the Spirit was given to select individuals for specific tasks (see Num 11:24-30). But according to Joel, a day would come when no distinction would be made on the basis of race, sex, age, nationality or social position. All the people of God would receive his Spirit with all the various gifts. This would, no doubt, bring a deep sense of fulfillment and joy to believers and judgment to nonbelievers.

Question 4. Joel isn't clear about the relationship between the offer of salvation (2:32) and the promise of the Spirit (2:28-29), although they obviously seem to be related. Peter, however, clearly states that those who receive salvation also receive the Spirit (Acts 2:38-39).

Question 5. We may view this as a prophecy that *has* been fulfilled, *is* being fulfilled in the church today, and *will* be fulfilled in that great and final Day of the Lord.

Question 6. The Lord states that he will enter into judgment in the Valley of Jehoshaphat (v. 2). Although there was a Valley of Jehoshaphat in the fourth century A.D., there is no evidence that there was literally such a place in Joel's day. *Jehoshaphat* means "the Lord judges." The point is that all the nations will be gathered together for judgment.

Question 7. The battle itself is an expression of the Lord's judgment. Joel isn't clear about whether the nations are destroying each other in battle or whether their destruction is a result of divine intervention. Either way, it is clear that the blood of the nations will flow freely because of God's judgment (see Rev 14:14-20).

Question 10. God uses his people to be a blessing to the nations. Judgment comes against those who hinder that work through God's people. God continues to be faithful to his children of the covenant (see Acts 3:25-26).

Study 8. The Lord Roars from Zion. Amos 1:1—2:16.
Purpose: To consider why the Lord's wrath was against Israel and its enemies.
Question 2. The Lord's roar may have been like a lion or like the roar of a thunderstorm. It is interesting to note that the Lord's roar comes from Jerusalem, the site of the temple in the southern kingdom of Judah, and not from any of the northern religious centers. But although the roar comes from Jerusalem, it causes drought in the northern kingdom, where Mount Carmel is located.

Questions 3-5. Amos begins by prophesying against the pagan nations surrounding Israel. We may imagine the people smugly agreeing with him, since most of these countries represented enemies and were threats at one time or another. Next, he turns to the southern kingdom of Judah. The division between Israel and Judah had caused deep wounds which were never completely healed, and so Joel's prophecy against Judah would probably be welcomed by those in Israel. But as the masterful preacher turns and shouts, "For three sins of *Israel,* even for four, I will not turn back my wrath" (v. 6), the people would be caught in what has been described as Amos's "coil of condemnation."

Question 8. This is the first time Amos has mentioned *the law of the Lord* and *his decrees.* The Lord judges people according the light he has given them.

Questions 9-10. Think of categories such as oppression, injustice, immorality and so on.

In verse 7 Amos says: "Father and son use the same girl and so profane my holy name." Evidently, the Israelites had adopted some of the practices of the Canaanite fertility religions and as a result had temple prostitutes. However, it is also possible that Amos is speaking against incest.

In verse 8 Amos mentions: "They lie down beside every altar on *garments taken in pledge.* This was a violation of the Jewish law which stated, "If you take your neighbor's cloak as a pledge, return it to him by sunset, because his cloak is the only covering he has for his body. What else will he sleep in?" (Ex 22:26-27).

Nazirites (v. 12) were not to cut their hair or drink wine. They were living reminders to Israel of being set apart for God.

Question 11. Between questions 10 and 11, you might ask the group to compare the lifestyle we enjoy as Americans and the lifestyle of those Amos spoke to, and ask what effect that lifestyle has on others.

If you choose to discuss this, you might mention the following. According to Arthur Simon, author of *Breaking Bread with the Hungry,* "One out of eighteen people in the world live in the U.S. That one eighteenth of the world's population, it so happens, gathers 35% of the world's income, 20% of humanity (basically Europe and America) controls 80% of the world's resources, which leaves 80% of the world's population to divide the remaining fraction of the world's resources" ([Minneapolis: Augsburg Publishing House, 1971], p. 23). The book *Rich Christians in an Age of Hunger* by Ronald Sider (IVP) would be an excellent resource for discussing this topic.

Question 13. Encourage the group to picture what Amos describes in these verses.

Study 9. Israel's Punishment. Amos 3:1-15.

Purpose: To understand that greater privileges bring greater responsibility—

and the possibility of greater judgment.

Question 2. You may wish to have the group discuss the difference between election and divine favoritism. It is important to remember that these people were originally "chosen" to be a blessing to all nations.

Question 4. Amos speaks of visible signs to warn the people. When the lion roars, the prey will be attacked; when the trumpet sounds, the people prepare for war; when the Lord speaks, the people have been warned.

Question 5. God has always provided his people with myriad opportunities of escape from forthcoming judgment by getting his message across through his chosen "mouthpieces."

Question 6. From this vantage point the sins of the people could be viewed. (See also Amos 4:1; 6:1.)

Question 8. Many times shepherds saw the meager remains of one of their animals after it had been devoured by a predator. Amos uses this experience to portray the meager remains of God's chosen people.

"Those who sit . . . on the edge of their beds and . . . on their couches" (v. 12) refers to the idle luxury of the rich.

Question 9. Amos is saying that people will come to grasp the horns of the altar and will find nothing to grab! This is a vivid way of saying that there will be no refuge from the Lord's judgment because of the severity of Israel's sins.

One of Israel's sins involved incorporating elements of paganism into their worship, especially by setting up a worship site in Bethel (v. 14).

Question 12. You may desire to have members share and pray as a group after considering their responses silently or after writing them on pieces of paper.

Study 10. Prepare to Meet Your God! Amos 4:1-13.

Purpose: To grasp that God disciplines us in order to bring us back to him.

Question 2. According to J. A. Motyer, women were "the final guardians of morals, fashions, and standards." By using women as the example here, Amos has isolated the heartbeat of Israel's society *(The Message of Amos* [Downers Grove, Ill.: InterVarsity Press, 1974], p. 93).

Question 3. In verse 2 the statement "The Sovereign LORD has sworn by his holiness" adds tremendous weight to the message which follows. If Israel continues in sin, certain consequences are inevitable.

Question 4. Jeroboam I, the first king of the Northern Kingdom, broke the law of Moses by establishing worship centers at Bethel and Dan. He was concerned that his subjects would go to Jerusalem and be won back to David's house. He later set up golden bulls in the sanctuaries, thus opening the door for the influence of Baal worship. Priests refused to serve at these new altars, so Jeroboam hired his own priests with little concern for their qualifications.

The reign of Jeroboam II, a contemporary of Amos (785-744 B.C.), was marked with the same kind of idolatry as his predecessor. By this time worship was not only going on at Bethel and Dan but also at subsidiary temples at Gilgal and Beersheba.

Question 6. Look for words such as *famine* (v. 6), *drought* (vv. 7-8), *blight* (v. 9), *plagues* (v. 10) and *defeat* (v. 11).

Question 7. It isn't necessary to read Deuteronomy aloud. Simply have people quickly scan its contents, looking for similarities between the judgments mentioned there and in Amos. The point of this question is to realize that God's judgments were not arbitrary. Both the curses for disobedience and the blessings for obedience were clearly identified in the Law. Prophets such as Amos, therefore, were not announcing something new. They were simply enforcing the provisions of God's covenant with Israel.

Question 8. Help the group to notice the repetition of the phrase *yet you have not returned to me* (vv. 6, 8, 9, 10, 11). God's judgments were not simply punishment for sin but were designed to bring the people back to him. Unfortunately, they refused to respond.

Question 12. Be sure to view this hymn in the context of God's threat of judgment. How might this description of God strike fear in the hearts of the people?

Study 11. Seek the Lord and Live! Amos 5:1—6:14.

Purpose: To see the grief of a just God as he urges his people to seek him.

Question 2. God had promised Abraham that his descendants would be as numerous as the stars in the sky (Gen 15:5). But Amos declares that Israel will be like a virgin who died childless. This would be a shocking statement to the Israelites.

Question 5. The first part of this question is merely factual and shouldn't require much discussion. The second part, however, requires a good deal of thought and provides a natural transition to question 6.

Question 6. Ask for specific examples that are parallel to those discussed in the previous question but which are also suited to our culture and circumstances.

Question 8. You may wish to ask the group to note the specific terms used in these verses.

The word *roll* (v. 24) derives from the same Hebrew word as "Gilgal" (v. 5). Gilgal was the place where the Israelites were circumcised after entering the Promised Land, the place where the Lord "rolled away the reproach of Egypt" from them (Josh 5:9). Amos declares that justice should now roll like a river in Israel rather than the empty religion of Gilgal.

Question 10. Notice that Israel is condemned in verse 6 not for what they had done but for what they had *failed* to do. This is one of the serious problems which results from being complacent (v. 1) about our Christian lives.

Study 12. Five Visions (Part 1). Amos 7:1—8:14.

Purpose: To realize that failure to respond to God's Word results in judgment and leads to an inability to hear God's Word.

Question 2. The group should be able to quickly identify the visions of locusts (vv. 1-2), fire (v. 4) and plumb line (vv. 7-9). After they have identified these visions, ask them to describe the first two. The third vision will be discussed more fully in question 5.

You may wish to point out one important item to the group. In the one hundred verses in Amos 1—6, the title *the Sovereign Lord* (RSV "the Lord GOD") is used only nine times. However, in the last three chapters the title is used eleven times in only forty-six verses. Amos is stressing the fact that the Sovereign Lord has the power to carry out his threats and promises.

Question 3. Some members of the group may wonder how a God who never changes could "relent." It isn't necessary to get into a detailed theological discussion on the nature of God. It is sufficient to point out that Scripture affirms that God responds to our prayers and that they seem to have a real effect on the outcome of events. For other examples, you might mention Genesis 18:22-33, where Abraham intercedes for Sodom and Gomorrah, and Exodus 32:9-14, where Moses intercedes for Israel.

Question 5. If anyone in the group has used a plumb line, ask them to explain what it is and what it's used for. If no one has had this experience, you might explain that a plumb line is a line with a weight attached at the end. It is used for determining whether a structure is truly vertical.

Question 9. Here again we see the language of a farmer/shepherd addressing an agrarian people. Harvest was very important to the Hebrew people, as it is to any culture. Three seasons of harvest occurred during the year in Palestine: the barley harvest (April-May), the wheat harvest (June-July) and the ingathering of the fruits in the fall. This image is used by Amos to emphasize the abundance of sin among God's people.

Question 10. Throughout the Old Testament the Hebrews' treatment of the widow, the orphan, the poor, the sojourner and the Levite are used as a barometer to indicate the condition of their relationship to God.

Question 11. This question covers a lot of verses, so don't feel that you must cover every detail in every verse. Instead, encourage the group to summarize the judgments Israel will experience.

Dan (v. 14) was one of the locations for an idolatrous calf set up by Jeroboam to maintain political control in the northern kingdom (1 Kings 12:28-30). The worship of the goddess Ashimah, prevalent among foreign settlers in Samaria, was also creeping into the religion of God's people. Evidently these changes were viewed as simply characteristics of the times with no harm intended to the faith. But the Lord viewed them as idolatrous.

Question 12. This question can be answered fairly easily, so feel free to move quickly to the next question, which will take more time to answer.

Question 13. In the Parable of the Sower (Mt 13) Jesus warns that those who respond to his message will be given more, and those who fail to respond will lose their opportunity to respond. In other words, we can become spiritually calloused and insensitive if we fail to respond to the light that is given to us. This is a great danger in the church today.

Study 13. Five Visions (Part 2). Amos 9:1-15.

Purpose: To see that hope, not judgment, is God's final word to Israel and to us.

Question 2. Unfortunately, older versions of the NIV have a different translation of verse 1 than that found in newer versions. The older version says: "Strike the tops of the pillars so that the thresholds shake. *Cut off the heads* of the people." The new version says: "Strike the tops of the pillars so that the thresholds shake. *Bring them down on the heads* of the people." The latter version gives a much better picture of what happens when the temple collapses.

The temple mentioned in verse 1 is probably not the temple in Jerusalem but rather symbolizes the religion of the northern kingdom. The vision emphasizes that idolatry leads to judgment.

Question 4. *Cush* (v. 7) occupied the territory south of Egypt and was the "Ethiopia" of classical writers. Evidently it was considered an insignificant nation in the ancient Near East. The Israelites would be shocked to learn that they were no better than the Cushites. They would also be shocked to learn that the Lord had guided the migration of the Philistines and the Arameans, just as he had led Israel from Egypt. The exodus was the primary redemptive event in Israel's history, and they considered it (and themselves) unique.

Questions 5-6. After so many prophecies of doom, Amos's words in verses

8-15 seem out of place to some scholars. However, Amos does not offer hope to Israel as a whole but rather to the faithful remnant within the nation (vv. 9-10).

Question 8. Since this is a very personal question, you might encourage the group to share by giving an example from your life. A further reference to use might be Romans 8:28.

Question 11. Be sure to leave enough time for this question, since it allows the group to reflect on what they have learned from these three prophetic books.

Doug Haugen is director of lay ministry at Bethlehem Lutheran Church in Auburn, California, and a freelance author. Doris Haugen is a public-school teacher and a Bible study leader.